Marooned

Marooned

THE STRANGE BUT TRUE ADVENTURES OF ALEXANDER SELKIRK,

the Real Robinson Crusoe

by Robert Kraske

Illustrated by Robert Andrew Parker

Clarion Books ☞ New York

Clarion Books
a Houghton Mifflin Company imprint
215 Park Avenue South, New York, NY 10003
Text copyright © 2005 by Robert Kraske
Illustrations copyright © 2005 by Robert Andrew Parker

The text was set in 12-point Berkeley.
Maps by Kayley LeFaiver.

www.houghtonmifflinbooks.com

Printed in the U.S.A.

Library of Congress Cataloging-in-Publication Data

Kraske, Robert.
Marooned : the strange but true adventures of Alexander Selkirk, the
real Robinson Crusoe / by Robert Kraske.
p. cm.
  Includes bibliographical references.
  ISBN 0-618-56843-3
1. Selkirk, Alexander, 1676–1721. 2. Survival after airplane accidents,
shipwrecks, etc.—Juan Fernández Islands. 3. Defoe, Daniel,
1661?–1731. Robinson Crusoe—Sources. I. Title.
  G530.S42K73 2005
  996.1′ 8—dc22
          2004028769

ISBN-13: 978-0-618-56843-7
ISBN-10: 0-618-56843-3

VB 10 9 8 7 6 5 4 3 2 1

To four young adventurers—
Nicholas, Michael, Benjamin,
and Abram

Contents

Mr. Selkirk would be going ashore—alone.

Selkirk's Choice

September 1704

*D*ark peaks rising from the sea. That was the first view of Juan Fernández. As the *Cinque Ports* entered Great Bay, the island appeared more welcoming—a half-moon beach, grassy valleys, wooded foothills, waterfalls plunging from high mountains. At the foot of cliffs, fur seals sunned on rocks and played in the surf.

The island was a welcome landfall, but the crew was watchful, uneasy. Juan Fernández was a Spanish island, and the *Cinque Ports* flew an English flag. Because England and Spain were at war, the island was not a safe place for an English ship. Spanish warships from the mainland sometimes stopped at the island. The *Cinque Ports,* needing to refill water casks and woodbins, risked being the target of a patrolling Spanish man-of-war.

At this remote island in the South Pacific, the conflict in Europe seemed far away. A quarrel among the ruling powers about who should sit on the Spanish throne had erupted into the War of the Spanish Succession. England and Holland, on one side, and Spain and France, on the other, were the major combatants.

Spain immediately banned English ships from its ports in Europe and South America. England's Queen Anne quickly struck back, declaring that English merchant ships could attack Spanish and French ships at sea and carry their valuable cargos back to England.

These English merchant ships were called privateers. They were armed vessels, privately owned, and licensed by the English government. Spain and France called them pirates. If captured, the crews would hang.

One of many privateers that set out from England was the *Cinque Ports*. For years it had carried cotton, sugar, and timber between English ports.

When the war began in 1701, the owners hired carpenters to convert the *Cinque Ports* from a cargo carrier to a privateer. Gun ports were sawed into its sides. Racks were built to hold cutlasses, daggers, and boarding axes. Deep in the hull a tin-lined room was constructed to store gunpowder. Finally, twenty cannons and cases of muskets were hoisted on board.

Few of the *Cinque Ports*'s crew—former bakers, barbers, cobblers, tinsmiths, tailors, fiddlers, haymakers, peddlers, thieves, and more—had ever been to sea before. All were eager to escape the poverty of their lives ashore. Adventure lured them, the chance to get rich on Spanish gold.

Among the few trained seamen on board were Captain Thomas Stradling and the sailing master, Alexander Selkirk.

Little is known about Stradling. He was twenty-one years of age and thought to be a gentleman of the upper class, but this was not known for sure. What the crew did know was that he was aloof, unfair, a bully. Once, during the voyage, they revolted against him. Whatever the cause, the matter was settled and the crew resumed its duties. Stradling liked to walk the deck with the ship's mascot, a monkey, on his shoulder.

Unlike the captain, Selkirk, the second in command, mixed easily with the men. On calm evenings he often joined them for a pint of flip—beer mixed with rum, sweetened with sugar, best served hot. Often he quarreled with Stradling about running the ship. After one heated argument, Stradling ordered him locked in a storeroom. It was Selkirk who had led the crew in the revolt.

Selkirk was a veteran seaman. At fifteen years of age, he had run away from home, the seaside village of Largo, Scotland. He sailed on merchant ships between the West Indies and England and learned navigation, which enabled him to become a ship's officer.

It was Selkirk who, as sailing master in 1703, had piloted the *Cinque Ports* from England south through the Atlantic Ocean, around stormy Cape

Horn, into the Pacific Ocean, north along the South American coast as far as Panama, and finally south again to Juan Fernández. The island lies 360 miles due west of Valparaiso, Chile, on the South American coast.

Primitive instruments were used at the time to guide a ship across the seas. Maps were unreliable. Some placed islands three hundred miles from their true position. Selkirk's ability to guide the *Cinque Ports* to a remote island in the broad Pacific demonstrated his skilled seamanship. (On another voyage, England's foremost navigator had missed the island by miles.)

He was twenty-seven years old and strongly built—"husky, a sturdy physique," allowed one writer. He also possessed a quick temper.

So far, the hunt for Spanish and French merchant ships along the South American coast had not gone well for the *Cinque Ports*. Only three small traders had been captured. They carried tobacco, timber, rope, and turtle shell. From one a small chest of gold coins was recovered. Then a French merchant ship gave up sacks of flour and sugar, a few casks of wine and brandy, and thirty tons of quince marmalade.

The crew grumbled. Halfway around the world to capture marmalade for their biscuits! More than that, they complained about water running low and the galley stove needing firewood. Hot food kept up spirits and courage.

The *Cinque Ports* headed for Juan Fernández, the only anchorage and watering place that could be chanced along the Spanish-held South American coast.

While water casks were being refilled from fresh-water streams on shore and trees cut for the wood-bin, Selkirk inspected the ship. After its long passage from England to Juan Fernández, many repairs were needed.

Careening a ship was the usual thing to do: towing it to shore, running lines from the masts to trees, hauling it over on its side. Timbers in the hull, holed and weakened by the woodboring teredo worm, could then be replaced.

There were cracks in masts and spars to brace, tears in sails to mend, gaps between deck planks to stuff with oakum and seal with pitch, fresh leather suction heads to replace those on the pumps worn from flushing water from the bilge.

Stradling, though, would hear none of it. Repairs could take days; a careened ship was helpless. Spanish warships could appear any day, any hour. As soon as water casks and wood for the galley stove came aboard, they would raise anchor and leave the sheltered bay.

Selkirk argued that Stradling was overly cautious. The risk had to be accepted. Patrolling warships were few and far between, and the ship was unfit to sail. A storm could swamp them, sending the ship to the bottom. His life, Stradling's life, the lives of the crew were at risk.

Stradling refused to yield. He intended to sail north along the South American coast, hunt merchant ships, then ambush the Manila galleon off Mexico. This Spanish treasure ship, heavily loaded with gold and silver and precious jewels, traveled only once each year from the Philippines to

Acapulco. Time was running short. They had to be on station by December to wait for the galleon to appear.

There would be no change of plan. His order stood.

Selkirk stubbornly refused to accept the decision. Now his well-known temper began to rise. He turned to the crew, his mates. They had stood together once before against the captain. The time had come again. He would choose the island—"to take [my] fate in this place [rather] than in a crazy vessel, under a disagreeable commander!"

Who among them would join him?

The men hesitated. Trade the ship for an island? Not one stepped forward.

Stradling may have seen an opportunity in Selkirk's reckless boast, a way to get rid of his troublesome sailing master. He decided to call Selkirk's bluff. He ordered Selkirk's sea chest brought on deck, along with a musket from the arms locker and meat and biscuits from the galley.

Lower the longboat, he commanded. Mr. Selkirk would be going ashore—alone.

Selkirk sits in the bow of the longboat. Two crewmen haul on the oars. Stradling, at the stern, hands on the tiller, steers.

The longboat grinds on the beach. Selkirk steps onto the island. The oarsmen lift the sea chest and place it on the stones. Carefully they set a bag of bullets and a bag of powder on top, along with a kerchief tied up with food, and lean the musket against the chest.

The boat shoves off.

On shore Selkirk waits. Perhaps he regrets his hot-tempered boast. Wading into the shallows, water to his knees, he "calls after his comrades," pleads to be taken back.

Stradling turns, shouts taunts, jeering at his difficult mate, no doubt glad to be free of him.

The oarsmen stroke the longboat toward the ship.

Hours pass. Then the *Cinque Ports*'s anchor lifts. Sails rise and fill with an offshore breeze. The former sailing master watches his ship round a point of land. Then it is gone.

Waves wash the rocks. The sun sinks in the west behind the island's jagged peaks. The dark forest looms. Far across the water, fur seals howl and croak. Alexander Selkirk, mariner, is about to face surviving alone on an isolated island in the South Pacific. Yet, still mulling events that placed him on the stony beach, he is unaware of his predicament.

"[My] heart yearned within [me], and melted at parting with
[my] comrades and all human society at once."

From the Beach to the Cave

he crew of the *Cinque Ports* were tough, hard men. They had to be to survive the long passage from England. They endured fierce storms around Cape Horn that battered the hull, opened seams between planks, and blew men tending sails into the raging sea. They suffered disease from the lack of fresh food and drank water so putrid and foul smelling that it had to be strained through kerchiefs to remove the green slime from the water casks. Holding the nose also helped. Hardships were part of the voyage.

Stradling's decision to maroon his sailing master was a harsh punishment, but not uncommon in those days. It was done to maintain discipline. Selkirk himself had witnessed a ship's officer marooned for some infraction of rules on a deserted island in the Cape Verde Islands in the eastern Atlantic. And pirates were said to force an offender onto a sandbar at low tide with only a one-shot pistol. His choice: the pistol or the sharks that came with the rising tide.

So Selkirk, understanding the hard discipline of shipboard life, may have accepted his difficult situation. "[My] heart yearned within [me]," he would later reveal, "and melted at parting with [my] comrades and all human society at once."

But this was uttered in years to come, in the warmth and comfort of a London coffeehouse. As the night came on, it's unlikely that he was deeply distressed. He believed that the whole episode, the dispute with Stradling, had been an unfortunate fit of temper on both their parts. His marooning on the island would be temporary—a day, a week, and the *Cinque Ports* would come back. Stradling needed him to help run the ship. Besides, he was the sailing master, the navigator, the one man able to sail the poorly charted ocean and find the way back to England. He would just have to make the best of it until the ship returned.

Still, he was alone, and he had to think of his safety. He considered building a fire but decided against it. Savages might see the flames. Old seafarers told of flesh eaters on South Pacific islands. An eyewitness to the practice was the famous Sir Francis Drake, one of the first to sail around the world. At one island he had watched helplessly from his ship offshore while natives roasted and ate captured crewmen.

Selkirk rammed a charge of powder and a bullet into the barrel of his flintlock musket. On guard, he waited, fighting off sleep.

Morning sun advancing across the bay awakened him. He grabbed the musket. But there was no alarm. The sun lighted the green slopes behind him. Trails of fog filled wooded ridges leading to the high mountains.

He looked across the bay. No white sails, no ship working around the headland into the bay. Stradling, taking out his revenge, would delay returning. Selkirk decided to wait, not move from the beach, not risk missing the ship.

He was hungry and looked at the biscuits and chunks of salt beef brought yesterday from the ship. Beef kept in casks for weeks often became so hard that the crew carved it into tobacco boxes. But this chunk might be edible. By habit he probably tapped a biscuit on a rock. There were those who said it was best to discard any biscuit from which tiny beetles failed to emerge: Not fit for a weevil, not fit for a man.

His sea chest held a few linen shirts and wool stockings, flint and steel for making fire, cooking pot, brass spyglass, hatchet, knife, a flask of rum, and a leather sack of gold coins—what good were they now? There were the Bible and books of devotion given to him by his mother back in Largo, and his books on navigation and geometry.

He also found his pint jar for taking his daily ration of flip. The words on its brown stone surface read:

> Alexander Selkirk, this is my [own].
> When you me take on board of ship
> Pray fill me with punch or flip.

His musket and leather bags of powder and bullets made up the rest of his worldly goods.

He spent the day on the beach, spyglass in hand. He knew from charts that the island was about twelve miles long and four wide. Sheer cliffs ringed most of the bay.

His spyglass picked out fur seals floating on the water or sunning themselves on rocks on the far shore. He could hear their faint barks. The adult seals were brown; the younger ones had black fur.

He ate another meal of biscuit and beef, washed down with water from a stream running from the forest into the sea. The light across the bay changed as the sun settled behind the high mountains. By the morrow the ship would surely return. All differences would be forgotten in the common goal of capturing Spanish gold.

The last biscuits and beef eaten, Selkirk walked the beach hunting for something edible. In the shallows he found crabs, mussels, and clams. Prying the shells open with his knife, he ate the soft flesh raw and sucked the juice.

He spotted lobsters crawling among the rocks. They were much larger than the lobsters he had caught as a boy in Largo. Some were three feet long. He reached into knee-deep water, grabbed one by its hard shell, and flipped it onto the shore. He bashed it with a rock, then tore the critter leg from body and chewed the stringy flesh.

By afternoon, however, he felt the effects of the uncooked meat. He barely pulled down his breeches before his bowels loosened.

In the morning he felt better, but again hungry. No white sails had appeared in the bay. He decided to prepare a proper meal.

He placed rocks in a circle and shaved kindling from dry sticks. Sparks from striking steel and flint drew a wisp of smoke. Gently he blew into the smoke until a tiny flame appeared. He filled the kettle with water from the stream, gathered clams and mussels, and caught another lobster. Tossing the fresh meat into the boiling water, he made a thick soup.

His stomach took more kindly to the hot, cooked food, although he lacked salt and pepper to season it.

With little else to do, he sat on his sea chest or in

the shade of trees bordering the beach to watch the broad entrance to the bay. The cold Peru Current, flowing north, kept the island free of tropical heat.

On the beach was a makeshift hut—sandalwood poles covered by sailcloth—made by firewood cutters and the watering party from the *Cinque Ports* as a shelter against sun and rain. He moved his sea chest into this rickety shelter.

Weeks passed and the *Cinque Ports* had not appeared in the bay to rescue him.

Had Stradling marooned him? Was it possible the ship would not return to Juan Fernández?

Selkirk's mood was dark. The island itself contributed to his low spirits. He would later reveal how "dejected, languid, and melancholy" he had begun to feel, "scarce able to refrain from doing [myself] violence."

Lonely beyond belief, he picked up his musket. It was still loaded with powder and a single shot, his defense against savages who had never appeared. One pull of the trigger would solve the problem of being alone. Was this why Stradling had ordered the musket? he must have wondered. Sweet revenge on his rebellious mate who dared question his orders?

Shaking, he thrust the musket clattering onto the rocks and made the decision to live.

After weeks on the beach, Selkirk decided he needed better shelter. The open hut of poles and sailcloth was too flimsy to protect against wind and blowing rain.

Caves above a line of trees offered a possibility. Trudging up the wooded slope, he looked into each one. The opening of the cave he chose was ten feet high. The ferns and weeds growing from the walls didn't appeal, but the hollow entrance offered a special advantage: a high lookout over the bay, a place to watch for a ship.

He carried his sea chest and few belongings up from the beach. Gathering ferns, he spread them on the rocky floor to form a mattress.

In front of the cave he piled rocks. Then he cut thorny branches from bushes and arranged them in front of the rocks. The rock wall, the thorns, and a bright fire at the entrance would hold wild beasts at bay. (Selkirk was as yet unaware that the most ferocious animals on the island were goats.)

The cave offered shelter from wind and rain but was damp and uncomfortable. In the mornings his arms and face were often dusted with dirt that had sifted down. A rain shower during the day might cause the ferns and weeds to drip cold water at night. It's likely he was frequently chilled, thus adding to his misery.

No matter how poorly he felt, though, hunger forced him from the cave each day on a desperate search for food. Sometimes he dug roots to boil into a broth. He tasted cautiously—especially when he found wild berries or bird eggs—fearful of making himself sick or even poisoning himself.

On the beach he spotted a sea turtle crawling from the water. Flipping the creature onto its back, he quickly dispatched it with his hatchet. Cutting tender meat into strips, he hung them in the sun to dry. The sweet meat provided a welcome relief from his diet of lobster, clams, and mussels.

Hunger was a daily problem, but so was the heavy silence of the island, especially at noon, when the sun was high. When loneliness grew too heavy, he emerged from the cave, singing hymns he had learned as a boy in the Presbyterian church in Largo. "There's an end of an auld [old] song," he shouted defiantly as a hymn ended, then beginning another.

He prayed aloud, bearing "up against melancholy and the terror of being left alone in a desolate place," and wept helplessly, half mad from the solitude. He feared his mind was slipping. He longed to hear a human voice.

He slept whole days away. Sleep was his only escape. Awake, he whistled Scottish folk tunes, a human sound in the island's stillness.

In the cave, gazing into the firelight, Alexander Selkirk may have thought of his family in Largo. Come to the shop, learn the business, his father, John, had offered. But cobbling shoes for the villagers and harnesses for their horses didn't appeal. That was why he had run away to sea.

His last day at home had not been pleasant. He had fought with his feeble-minded brother, Andrew. When he asked the boy to fetch a pail of water from the well, Andrew brought seawater from the bay.

Alexander gagged and sputtered. Furious, he grabbed a walking staff, swatted the giggling boy, and was wrestled to the floor by his father.

Neighbors reported a "tumult" in the house, his cousin John Howell later recorded. Church elders ordered Alexander to appear "before the face of the congregation" and scolded him for his "scandalous behavior." Humiliated, he made "public acknowledgment of his sin" and promised to mend his ways.

That was how he remembered Andrew.

His mother, Euphan, a loving woman who had given him the Bible to accompany him on his travels, likely brought tender thoughts. What would she think now if she could see him with a scraggly beard, sitting in a cave, staring into a fire burning bright against wild animals? . . .

Late one night he was startled awake by savage sounds—growls, snorts, barks, bellows—coming from the beach. He threw sticks on the fire, grabbed the musket, and crouched against the cave wall. Night magnified his terror—he could barely see over the flames into the darkness. An onshore breeze carried a sickening stench, like dead fish rotting in the sun.

Daylight revealed the source of the awful sounds. During the night hundreds of seals had invaded the beach. In the bay he could see more heads swimming toward shore. Juan Fernández was the island the animals returned to each year to breed and give birth to their young.

Their "dreadful howlings," he would later recall, were too terrible for human ears.

With the beach occupied for weeks by the seals—"they lin'd the shore very thick for above half a mile"—he could no longer gather seafood. Still, hunger drove him daily from the cave. He had seen goats on the island—small, dark brown, with curled horns.

Accounts differ as to how Selkirk slew the first goat. One says he came unexpectedly upon the animal. It didn't move but stood still studying him. He picked up a downed tree limb and clubbed its head until it dropped.

Another account says he waited behind a tree near a stream, musket ready. When a goat, followed by three or four others, stepped toward the stream, he fired the musket's single shot. The wounded animal hobbled into the underbrush, and he scrambled after it. Grabbing it by the neck and a leg, he slammed the bleating animal to the ground, then carried the dead goat back to the cave.

In all likelihood hunger drove him to hurry his preparations—skinning the animal, plunging his hand into the warm carcass, pulling out the innards, hacking away the limbs, roasting the meat over a pimento-wood fire, prodding with a sharp stick to make it cook faster.

Gorging on the hot flesh, he could have been mistaken for the most primitive savage, squatting before the fire, tearing at the meat, chewing down to the white slick bones.

It was possible that he would stay here for years,
perhaps for the rest of his days.

Prisoner and Master

～

Sometime in May or June of 1705, after eight or nine months on the beach and in the cave, Selkirk admitted a hard truth. Stradling and the *Cinque Ports* would not be returning to the island. It was possible that he would stay here for years, perhaps for the rest of his days.

He made the decision, then, to build a shelter, a hut of some kind, warm and dry, and move out of the cave.

A site on the far side of the valley in a grove of

trees near a stream, "fanned with continual breezes and gentle aspirations of wind," appealed to him.

He chopped down young trees. The poles became frames for two huts. Goatskins, dried, scraped, and cleaned, formed the walls. Grass seven feet long from a nearby field, cut and tied with strips of goatskin and overlaid in bundles, provided a rainproof roof.

The largest hut was used for living. He built a fire pit from rocks and, from saplings, a crude chair, table, and bed frame. He hunted seals. Their soft fur provided his bedding.

The smaller hut became his smokehouse and kitchen. Here he circled stones for another fire pit and built rude boxes. He covered the boxes with goatskins weighted with rocks to protect food from rats, the offspring of rats from ships wrecked on the island's rocky shores.

Shelter taken care of, he began to explore the island. With a walking staff he hiked through groves of mountain ash and towering cottonwood trees with trunks twenty feet around. He discovered waterfalls and streams running down long slopes to the sea. The trees ended high on the slopes. He watched clouds butt and burst into shreds against the mountain peaks.

In humid valleys he found enormous ferns with leaves six to ten feet across. Spiders' webs hung round as wagon wheels between trees. He marveled at the island birds—hawks, owls, petrels, puffins, blackbirds, and two species of hummingbirds, "no bigger than a large humble bee [bumblebee]," one cinnamon color and the other bright green.

In one valley he came upon a field of turnips and stands of fig trees. He found patches of oats, pumpkins, radishes, parsnips, and parsley growing wild. Selkirk gathered the crops gratefully, but how they came to grow there he didn't know. (In 1591 Spanish settlers from the South American mainland had planted crops and grazed goats during a brief but unsuccessful attempt to farm and build homes on the island.)

Looking through his spyglass, he saw black-plum trees on high rocky slopes. But getting to the trees proved dangerous. The volcanic rock crumbled under

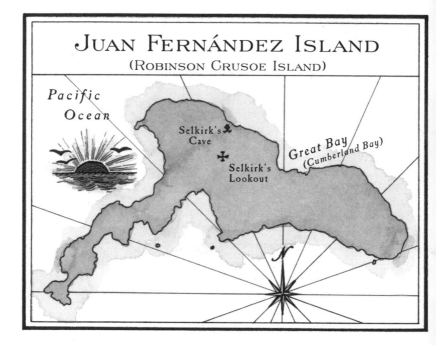

JUAN FERNÁNDEZ ISLAND
(ROBINSON CRUSOE ISLAND)

Pacific
Ocean

Selkirk's
Cave

Selkirk's
Lookout

Great Bay
(Cumberland Bay)

N

his feet. When he grasped a young tree to haul himself up a steep slope, he pulled it out, roots and all.

"The soil is a loose black earth," he later noted, "the rocks very rotten, so that, without great care, it is dangerous to climb the hills."

He filled his shirt with plums and took a safer route down.

One day he came upon a grove of cabbage palms. The "cabbage" grew from the center of leaves at the top of the palm. It was white and sweet to the taste. A leaf of cabbage became a substitute for bread.

Each day, spyglass in hand, he trekked to a high ridge overlooking the bay. There he scanned the horizon. But there were no sails to be seen, only the shining sea. He stacked dry grass and branches, ready to set on fire. The smoke would signal a passing ship.

But a signal fire also meant taking a fearful risk. The waters between Juan Fernández and the coast of South America were patrolled by Spanish and French warships. A smoke signal might bring one or the other. After months on the island, he decided to give himself up to the French but not to the Spanish. "[The Spanish] would murder him," he feared, "or make a slave of him in the [silver] mines."

He chose to take his chances with the French.

Despite his daily watch, no ship arrived to rescue him. He was alone, both master of the island and its prisoner.

He began to try different meals—salads, a soup of goat meat, turnips and cabbage flavored with herbs, roasted fish, boiled lobster with oatcakes, a jam made from plums and spread on a cabbage-palm leaf. A favorite was leg of goat flavored with herbs and eaten with palm cabbage.

He learned to season meat with a sweet pepper from the pimento tree, salt evaporated from seawater, and a black pepper called *malagita*. This last he found "very good to expel wind and against griping of the guts."

He carved spoons and forks from goat horns. A lucky find was a barrel washed onto shore. From the iron hoops holding the staves he forged knife blades and hooks for fishing. From chunks of a tree limb he hollowed bowls and cups.

When his flint and steel wore out, he found another way to build a fire. His knife blade striking a rock sent sparks into loose piles of thread pulled from his shirt or onto shavings of dried seaweed and driftwood.

Twirling a hardwood stick between his palms into soft pimento wood was another source of fire. The friction created a weak flame that he coaxed into a roaring blaze. The wood burned "very clear" and refreshed him "with its fragrant smell." It served both to warm his hut on cool evenings and as a light, bright as candles, by which to read his Bible—sometimes aloud to keep up his ability to speak—and books on geometry and navigation.

He found the Bible entirely different from what he had known as a boy in Largo. Then, he had resisted the harsh religion of the church elders. In the Scriptures, he now found comfort for his troubled thoughts, courage to face each day, acceptance of his strange fate on the island. His anger cooled. Reading in the morning and evening became a pleasant way to start and end his day.

Dawn brought the creation of a new day—a rose flush in the eastern sky, streaks of lemon and lavender, then a rim of sun rising above the horizon and the first spread of morning light washing sea and sky. A faint breeze might bring the scent of blossoms opening. On some mornings a rainbow arced from the mist across the broad valley.

Selkirk's days followed a regular routine. After a reading in the Bible, he prepared a light breakfast— fruit, a cabbage leaf, a drink of fresh water.

Next a bath in the nearby stream, scrubbing himself with pumice, a soft volcanic stone. He mashed charcoal from the fire pit into powder, placed a line on a finger, scrubbed his teeth, then rinsed his mouth in the stream. A crude comb constructed from slivers of pimento wood did little to tidy his unruly hair and beard.

Ahead awaited a day of ease and pleasant tasks. A walk on the beach might reward him with the capture of a sea turtle. He hung the meat to dry in the sun. One turtle shell he cleaned with coarse sand and polished with fine pumice. In the hut the shell, shaded by a large leaf, kept water cool. A dip with a clam shell brought a refreshing drink to his lips.

On some days he played in the waves—always cautious, though, to stay near shore when seals frolicked nearby. He remembered when a sailor from the *Cinque Ports,* mistaking their play for friendliness, had approached one. The frisky seal turned aggressive and fastened its teeth in the sailor's head. Hauled back on board, he died the same day.

On a raft built from the boles of young trees tied together with bark strips, he fished for snapper, bonito, sea bass, and yellowtails. His line was made from goat sinews—the strong cords that attach muscle to bone. A hook came from a piece of the iron barrel hoop he had found, properly sharpened and shined.

From the same iron hoop he fashioned the blade of a fish spear, pointed and polished with pumice and bound to a pole with strips of bark. He also made a two-foot blade and attached a handle carved from goat horn, handy for beating through brush.

Goats also provided a way to replace his torn clothes.

"I made [myself] a coat and cap of goat skins, which [I] stitched together with little thongs of the same, that [I] cut with my knife." He poked eyelets with a sliver of metal, ground to a point on stone, and joined the skins with sinew. Goatskin provided the material for leggings to protect against thorns and bushes and for a jacket and breeches.

As he grew to know his island, he felt more comfortable. "[I] came at last to conquer all the inconveniences of [my] solitude and to be very easy," he said.

But there were days when the island's quiet grew heavy. He had no living soul to talk to. Moody and dispirited, he wondered what God had in mind, imprisoning him on this remote island.

These melancholy periods, however, came about less and less as the weeks passed and his contentment continued to grow. He found his temper moderating. His angry outbursts at trees and sky for the injustice of his lot ceased.

He counted the days by cutting notches into tree limbs. Every seventh day he declared a Sunday and observed with special readings from the Bible.

The island's goats provided him with fresh meat. Came the day, though, when he fired his last bullet and finished the end of the meat salted and hung in his kitchen hut. Now he had no way to take an animal.

Walking near a stream one day, he spotted a young

goat. He dropped his walking staff and chased it. His running ability surprised him. Could he capture a full-grown goat?

At first he could catch only those goats he chased into a dead-end gully or onto a rocky crag. In those places the goat couldn't escape.

But as weeks passed, his "speed of foot" increased. When his shoes finally rotted and fell apart, he went without. The soles of his feet grew hard as leather.

"My way of living and continual exercise of running strengthen'd me, so that I ran with a wonderful swiftness thro the woods and up the hills and rocks, and was able to capture the strongest and nimblest goat inside a few minutes."

He lifted each bleating and struggling prize, slung it across his shoulders, and carried it to his kitchen hut where he had built a pen of strong sticks pounded into the ground.

Despite his growing ease on the island, it was an accident with a goat that showed him how alone he truly was.

Selkirk had chased the animal up a slope. The goat hid in a clump of bushes. He dove into the scrub and grabbed the goat, unaware that the bushes hid a ledge. Over he plunged, the goat in his arms.

Hours later, "stunned and bruis'd," he felt consciousness returning. Slowly he became aware that dusk was falling. The dead goat was under him. It had cushioned the shock of his fall.

He could barely move his head or lift an arm. Night came. He lay cold and alone in the dark.

In the morning he crawled down the slope to his hut "about a mile distant." There he "lay senseless for the space of three days." The fire burned low and went out. Without it, nights were dark and chill.

Ten more days passed before he could stand. It was a harsh lesson. He was reminded again that he was utterly alone. He had no one to depend on but himself.

As soon as he was able to move about, he caught several young goats and placed them in the pen. Who could tell? Another fall, an illness, might confine him to the hut. Unable to hunt food, he would grow weak and starve.

Sometime in mid-summer, sea lions waddled onto the beach to mate. Selkirk decided to find out if the meat of a sea lion was edible. If so, it would make a welcome change in his meals.

The sea lions were large. Some were monsters "above 20 feet long" and weighed not less than "two ton." They fought over the smaller seals by swatting one another with their heavy tails. The beasts were "capable of seizing or breaking the limbs of a man."

Gathering his courage, he approached a sea lion on the edge of the pack. It roared and charged "like an angry dog." Selkirk danced away.

Armed with his walking staff, he again approached, poking and swatting the animal across its tender nose, driving it back. As he edged closer, it charged again. But this time, instead of retreating, he dodged the clumsy charge and stepped alongside the beast between head and tail. The animal was unable to reach him with either jaws or thrashing tail.

Selkirk pulled his hatchet from his belt. A single blow to the back of the animal's head dropped it.

He had hoped for thick steaks. After roasting the flesh of the sea lion, however, he found it too oily to eat—the meat was buried under a seventeen-inch layer of fat. But the "hair of [its] whiskers was stiff enough to make exceedingly fine toothpickers."

Young seals, though, proved more to his taste, "as good as English lamb." Their boiled fat provided cooking oil. When cooled, it served as butter spread on a cabbage leaf.

By the end of his second year on Juan Fernández, Selkirk was living comfortably. Still, there was an annoying problem he hadn't solved: the island's rats.

Hidden during the day, they came out at night. Firelight and the scent of food lured them. He could hear their scurryings in the underbrush around the hut. Sometimes he could see their red eyes watching him. After he fell asleep, they crept into the hut, sniffed and nibbled his fingers and toes, and chewed his clothes.

There were also cats on the island; like the rats, they came from ships wrecked in the past. He tried to capture a few, but they eluded him, dashing into the underbrush as he approached.

Then, in an unexpected way, his problem with rats was solved.

While walking through the forest one day, he came upon a litter of newborn kittens between the roots of a large tree. Gathering them into his arms, he returned to his hut and placed them in the pen with the young goats.

Day after day he fed the kittens goat milk and scraps of goat meat. As they grew, they slept in the hut at night. The fearsome rats still eyed him from the darkness beyond the hut, but they stayed away.

In time a dozen cats roamed the hut. He enjoyed their company, talked to them, even selected his favorites. But secretly he was afraid of them. If he died in the hut, he believed, the cats would eat his body. The thought troubled him.

One day while on a high slope, Selkirk was startled to see the sails of two ships in the bay.

His heart leaped. Rescue! Dashing through the woods, leaping rocks and bushes, he ran down the slope calling and waving his goatskin cap.

On the beach men stepped from a boat, muskets in hand. They wore shiny metal helmets with narrow brims. Spanish soldiers!

For a long moment soldiers and marooned mariner stared at each other. Then Selkirk turned and fled. A musket ball breezed past his ear.

He ran into the forest, the Spanish soldiers chasing close behind. A gully lay in his path. Frantic with fear, he slid down and climbed the far side.

Running, stumbling, tripping through under-brush, he came to a tall cabbage palm. He scrambled up and hid among the broad leaves just as the soldiers appeared. There were six of them.

The soldiers took off their helmets and wiped their sweaty brows. Which way to go? Each pointed in a different direction. Then, no decision forthcoming, they decided to give up the chase. They undid their breeches and peed against the tree. From among the leaves Selkirk watched, terrified.

Then the soldiers picked up their muskets and

moved off. A few sharp reports and a painful bleating told Selkirk they had shot a goat. Then a few more shots. Meat for their ships.

The next day, hidden behind boulders on his high lookout, he watched the scene in the bay through his spyglass. Spanish seamen floated water casks out to the anchored warships. Soon anchors raised, sails unfurled, and the ships moved out of the bay.

Years later, seated in a warm coffeehouse in London, Selkirk was able to joke about his near capture and fortunate escape. "Their prize being so inconsiderable," he said of the Spanish soldiers, "it is unlikely they thought it worth while to be at great trouble to find it."

Dusk falls quickly in the tropics. But Selkirk no longer feared the night, nor did it still hold the phantoms of his imagination.

By the light of his pimento-wood fire, he held the forepaws of his favorite cat, dancing and singing sea songs and Scottish folk tunes. The other cats silently watched.

In a warm glow of contentment, he may have thought of his former shipmates aboard the *Cinque Ports*. What would they say about their sailing master dancing in the firelight with a cat! But he knew his answer. "I never danced with a lighter heart or greater spirit any where to the best of music than I did to the sound of my own voice with my dumb animals."

His life on Juan Fernández had become a daily joy, his days aboard ship and his home in Largo increasingly remote. The hut was warm, food plentiful. He was never bored. Knowledge of the island had replaced fear and ignorance. He had a sense of complete freedom, of fulfillment, of safe harbor. There was the solitude to endure, of course, and the lack of a mate or two to enjoy a pint of flip and a chat. But in this he had no choice.

He came to a decision. If fate decreed, he would be content to spend the rest of his days on his island kingdom, master of his own life and destiny.

On the night of January 31, 1709, another day ended, he lay down on his fur-seal bedding. His favorite cats came to curl at his feet. Others lay on a mat of sweet-smelling grass. Perhaps there was a moon that night and the bay was visible, flat as a black mirror, reflecting the moon's path.

The pimento-wood fire burned down to comforting embers. A swath of stars became visible through the trees. Far out on the darkling sea two ships sailed a course for Juan Fernández.

He was a strange sight—clothed in goatskins, beard hanging to his waist.

The *Duke* and *Duchess* Arrive

F rom his high lookout Selkirk watched the two ships enter the bay. He saw their flags through his spyglass: English!

He ran down the slope and through the woods. At the beach he thrust his hiking staff into his goatskin cap and waved frantically. A boat was lowered. As it neared shore, he heard English voices, saw English faces. Eight men waded ashore and pointed muskets at him.

He was a strange sight—clothed in goatskins, beard

hanging to his waist, unable to speak, managing only to grunt and mutter words that sounded like "marooned . . . marooned."

To the seamen he must have looked like a half-wit, a castaway too long alone, no doubt the survivor of a shipwreck. An officer pointed to the boat. Selkirk stepped in. The boat returned to the larger of the two ships.

Seamen crowded the rail and stared. The strange man climbed a rope ladder hung from the ship's side. The deck rose and fell on the long swells. He staggered, gripped the rail.

"At his first coming on board us," Captain Woodes Rogers commented, "he had so much forgot his language for want of use, that we could scarce understand him, for he seem'd to speak his words by halves."

Noting Selkirk's cap, breeches, and jacket of goatskin, Rogers said, "He looked wilder than the first owners of them."

He offered the castaway a cup of rum but was refused. After drinking only water and goat's milk on his island, Selkirk was sure rum would be too strong for his stomach.

Rogers ordered a plate of food. Selkirk's nose wrinkled in disgust. He would not touch the beef or the biscuits holed by weevils.

One of the officers, William Dampier, recognized Selkirk—"the best man on the *Cinque Ports*," he stated.

But Rogers had little time for the castaway. He was needed elsewhere. Nearly half the 225 men on the two ships were ill. It was the seamen's disease: scurvy. Weeks of feeding on salt beef and biscuits, and a lack of fresh fruit and vegetables, brought on pale skin, sunken eyes, infected gums, and loose teeth. Bleeding under the skin left red-and-black blotches. The men coughed constantly; their breath stank like sewage. (It was not yet known that the disease is caused by a lack of vitamin C, which is found in citrus fruits, tomatoes, potatoes, cabbage, and green peppers—food not generally available to seamen on long ocean voyages.)

The sick men were lifted from the lower deck on canvas slings—some still in their hammocks—and lowered over the side into boats. At the rail others patiently waited their turn.

Selkirk, in a frenzy of gratitude for being rescued,

made known to Rogers that he would go ashore and help care for the sick men.

He dashed up a slope and caught three goats. On the beach tents made from old sails were being set up for the suffering crewmen. There Selkirk built a fire and showed the crew how to roast the meat.

Leading a party of six seamen, he cut sweet-smelling grass for the sick men to lie on and gathered turnips, cabbages, sorrel, and watercress. With the fresh greens he used a large ship's kettle to make a gentle broth.

Within three days, Rogers saw his men gaining strength and struggling to their feet.

A seaman who had been a barber in England cut off Selkirk's beard and trimmed his shaggy hair and scraggly eyebrows. Selkirk selected clothes from the *Duke*'s stores—shirt, woolen stockings, breeches, shoes with buckles. But, having gone barefoot for so long, he found the shoes uncomfortable. "It was some time before he could wear shoes after we found him," Rogers noted. "For not being used to any for so long, his feet swelled when he came first to wear 'em again."

As the health of the crew improved, Rogers was able

to join Selkirk for meals on shore. Within days, Selkirk's ability to speak returned, and the two talked about the hazards of navigation. Juan Fernández, Rogers said, was "[a] small island, we [were] in some doubts of striking it. Not one chart agrees with another."

Intently he listened to the marooned mariner's tales of survival on the island. Selkirk impressed him as an interesting and likable man, pleasant to talk with. Selkirk confided that he "was a better [man] while in this solitude than ever . . . before."

Curious officers and men visited Selkirk's huts in the grove of trees. They found goatskins hung on the walls, matted grass on the floor, a turtle shell filled with fresh water and covered by a cabbage-palm leaf. No litter, like most seamen's lodgings, no untidiness. Altogether pleasant, cool, and shaded.

Rogers commanded the *Duke* and the *Duchess*, two privateers. He was thirty years of age, tall, well built, and self-assured. Unlike most captains, he respected his crew and addressed them courteously. Each day he insisted they attend Church of England services on the quarterdeck.

The crews of the two ships considered him a fine seaman and a fair and proper master. He also maintained strict discipline over his sometimes unruly men. One seaman who uttered mutinous remarks was bent over the capstan and whipped. Salt was then rubbed into the open wounds.

The two raiders had left Bristol, England, on August 2, 1708. In January 1709, after surviving high winds and towering waves around Cape Horn, they arrived at Juan Fernández battered and leaking. The *Duke* was Rogers's ship—80 feet long, 25 feet at the beam, with 30 five-inch guns and a crew of 117. The *Duchess* was slightly smaller: 26 guns, a crew of 108.

Twenty men could have sailed either ship, but extra hands were needed to take over captured ships and to replace those who died in battle or from disease.

Rogers intended to attack Spanish ships along the coast of South America. His plan was much like Stradling's nearly four and a half years earlier: to sail north so that, by November, his ships would be positioned off Mexico to intercept the grandest prize of all, the Manila galleon, the Spanish empire's treasure ship bound on its annual journey to Acapulco.

Before that battle could take place, though, the *Duke* and *Duchess* had to be repaired. While the sick men recovered in tents on the beach, Rogers ordered the heavy guns hoisted out of the hold, taken ashore, and pointed toward the bay entrance. There they would discourage patrolling Spanish warships from entering the bay.

The lightened ships were then towed into shallow water. Lines and pulleys strung between masts and trees on shore tipped the ships on their sides.

The bottoms were crusted with barnacles, which work parties burned off with torches. Carpenters replaced hull planks rotten with holes bored by teredo worms, then smeared on an oily mix of tar, tallow, and sulfur. The slick coating would keep the destructive worms and barnacles from attaching to the hull for a time and add speed in a sea chase after slower merchant ships.

While men labored on the hull, others mended torn sails and scrubbed slime from water casks.

Carpenters' mates cut trees for new yardarms to replace those cracked and split in the stormy passage around Cape Horn.

Another work party on shore caught seals and skinned and boiled them to extract eighty tons of oil "for the use of our lamps and to save our candles," Rogers said. The crew enjoyed baby seal. They agreed with Selkirk that the tender meat tasted like "English lamb" back home.

Selkirk helped supply the ships with fresh food. He led a work party to gather turnips, radishes, cabbages, and plums, and he pointed out the best places for fishing. Rogers noted that the men caught "several sorts, all very good: as silverfish, rockfish, pollock, oldwives, and crawfish in such abundance that in a few hours we could take as many as would serve some hundreds of men."

Each day the castaway captured two or three goats so their meat could be salted and stored in casks.

Watching Selkirk catch goats, Rogers suggested a contest. Who could capture a goat first? The crew's "nimblest runners"; the *Duke*'s mascot, an English bulldog called Lord Harry; or Selkirk?

He watched amazed as the marooned mariner ran into the trees and dashed up slopes. "He distanc'd and tir'd both the dog and the men, catch'd the goats and brought 'em to us on his back."

Selkirk's victory, Rogers believed, was due to his "plain and temperate way of living on the island"—fresh air, daily exercise, a variety of fresh fruits and vegetables, and no tobacco or "strong liquor."

As the repaired hulls were towed into deep water, pans of burning pitch were placed belowdecks. The fumes seeped into every corner, ridding the damp hulls of fleas, beetles, cockroaches, and rats—for a few weeks at least.

Repairs and restocking food, water, and woodbins took eleven days. Heavy cannons were hoisted over the rail from the ship's boats and placed behind closed gun ports.

As a final detail, Rogers may have ordered the deck painted red, a customary practice in those days of sailing ships armed with cannons. The paint would have been carried all the way from Bristol. In battle, blood spilled on the deck would not be so visible.

Learning that Selkirk had been sailing master of the *Cinque Ports* and a veteran seaman "of great skill and conduct who, having had his books with him, had improv'd himself much in navigation during his solitude," Rogers appointed him second mate of the *Duke*.

"Febr. 12," Rogers wrote in his journal. "This morning we . . . got the last wood and water aboard, brought off our men, and got everything ready to depart."

Raising anchor and setting sail two days later, the *Duke* and *Duchess* eased out of Great Bay.

As he went about his new duties that afternoon, the former castaway looked back on his island home. Four years and four months he had survived alone. He could point out the beach and cave where he had spent his nights, the lookout spot above the trees—so many days watching for a sail—the grove of trees concealing his two huts.

By evening the far-off mountains had slid below

the horizon. With the *Duchess* following astern, the two raiders headed north on the "Spanish lake"—the sea off the western shore of South America that Spain claimed for its own.

The Spanish gunners "did not ply their great guns half as fast as we did."

Pacific Adventures and the Manila Galleon

*R*ogers kept the *Duke* and *Duchess* about twenty miles out, just beyond the horizon from the South American mainland. On March 16, 1709, the two privateers came upon their first prize.

The ship was a small trading vessel. The threat of the *Duke's* open gun ports was enough to lower its sails.

The master, Antonio Heliagos, was brought on board the *Duke*. He was heading for a village along the coast to take on a cargo of flour, he told Rogers. Amazingly, Heliagos, half Indian and half Spanish, had unexpected news about Stradling and the crew of the *Cinque Ports*.

Four years earlier, Heliagos was cruising along the coast, farther north from where they were now. On the rocky shore he saw the wreck of a ship.

People from a nearby village told him the ship's name: the *Cinque Ports*. Strong winds had pushed it toward shore. The ship ran onto an underwater shelf, broke apart, and sank. Almost all the crew drowned, but the captain and six seamen made shore in a boat.

Soldiers were waiting. Arms tied behind their backs, the shipwrecked seamen were marched to the local jail. Then they were taken overland to Lima, Peru. After spending four years in prison, they were again moved—Heliagos didn't know where. He thought possibly Spain.

Selkirk was stunned. What if he had not gone ashore on Juan Fernández? He might have drowned or still be wasting away in a Spanish prison. By choosing the island, he had escaped a dreadful fate.

In the next two weeks three small traders gave up their cargos—soap, leather, cocoa, coconuts, timber, and tobacco. One of these traders Rogers renamed the *Increase*. He placed sick men from the *Duke* and *Duchess* aboard and made Selkirk master.

On April 2 the squadron's first large prize came into view. The 450-ton *Ascensión* was nearly half again the size of the *Duke*. A tactic Rogers may have used was to approach the merchantman upwind. The *Ascensión,* sails fluttering when wind was blocked from its sails, then slowed in the water. The *Duke* and *Duchess* closed in.

Now began a scare tactic intended to bully and terrify the Spanish crew. The blare of battle trumpets aboard the privateers and the hammering of drums foretold the coming attack. Gun ports opened and the ugly snouts of cannons poked through. Bare-chested seamen raised cutlasses and boarding axes. Others swung three-pronged grappling hooks, ready to hurl them at the merchantman's rail and haul the ships together.

THE *Long* Voyage Home
January 11, 1710 – October 14, 1711

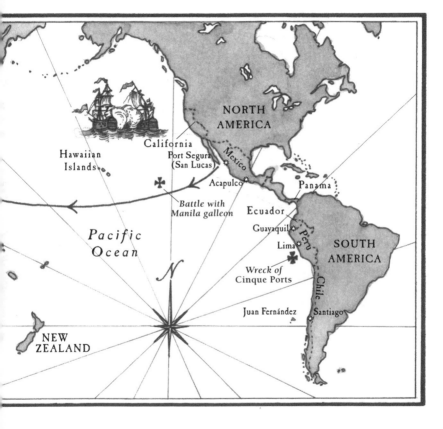

North America

Hawaiian Islands

California
Port Segura
(San Lucas)

Mexico

Acapulco

Panama

*Battle with
Manila galleon*

Ecuador

Guayaquil

Lima

Peru

South America

*Pacific
Ocean*

*Wreck of
Cinque Ports*

Chile

N

Juan Fernández

Santiago

New
Zealand

The display of might was enough for the *Ascensión*'s captain. He ordered the ship's flag lowered: Surrender.

"Tho' one of the largest merchant ships in these seas," Rogers recorded in his journal, "she deem'd herself so safe in the King of Spain's private ocean that no gun had ever been put aboard her to fire. Indeed, for arms I saw not so much as a pistol in her."

The *Ascensión* proved a valuable prize—320 bales of linens, woolens, and silks; boxes of knives, scissors, and hatchets; silver-handled swords; valuable snuff-boxes, silver shoe buckles, fine porcelain dinner plates; 30 tons of gold and silver religious medals, crosses, and crucifixes. Rich booty that would bring high prices in London.

Days later the squadron captured another big merchant ship, en route from Panama to Lima, Peru. Passengers on the *Havre de Grâce* were rich merchants. A search of their clothes and trunks uncovered bags of pearls and valuable jewels.

The *Havre de Grâce* carried twenty cannons. Six were mounted behind closed gun ports. The others were stowed in the hold. The befuddled commander had not expected English privateers in Spanish waters. Rogers ordered the cannons removed from the hold and mounted in empty gun ports. He renamed the ship the *Marquiss,* as he spelled it, and sent the passengers ashore.

Rogers's squadron was now made up of the *Duke, Duchess,* and *Marquiss;* Selkirk's small fifty-ton hospital ship, the *Increase;* and a second fifty-tonner captured off Peru, the *Joseph.*

The three privateers now boasted a total of seventy-six guns, enough to bully any foe.

Rogers sailed the fleet to the Gulf of Guayaquil on the coast of Ecuador.

Guayaquil was a wealthy town located on the Guayas River thirty-three miles upstream from the gulf. Merchant ships anchored in the gulf to unload their cargos onto barges. The barges were then rowed upriver to the town.

At midnight on April 17 Selkirk joined two hundred other crewmen on boats and headed up the alligator-infested river, "pester'd and stung grievously by muskitoes." The raid increased the expedition's loot by 23,500 gold pieces, 230 bags of flour, 150 bales of cloth, 1 ton of sugar, casks of fresh food, and barrels of gunpowder.

But the raiders took something else from the town. Within ten days of leaving the hot and humid area, Selkirk's hospital ship was caring for 180 seamen ill with tropical fever. Fortunately, the *Increase*'s captain escaped the sickness.

In November 1709, keeping to his timetable, Rogers and his squadron waited off the coast of Baja California. The three privateers formed a patrol line through which the Manila galleon would have to sail to reach the port of Acapulco. The *Duchess, Duke,* and *Marquiss* cruised fifteen, thirty, and forty-five miles off shore. Selkirk, now in command of the *Joseph*, was assigned to carry messages among the three.

On November 7 Rogers wrote in his journal: "Sir Thomas Cavendish, in Queen Elizabeth's time, took the Manila ship in this place on the 4th of November."

He was referring to the only capture of a Manila galleon, the *Santa Ana,* in 1587.

A two-masted ship, a "Manila galleon," was the largest and richest merchant vessel sailing the oceans. In June of each year since 1565, a Manila galleon set out from Manila in the Philippine Islands, bound for Acapulco, Mexico. Each treasure ship carried chests of gold and exotic trade goods from India, China, and Japan.

In Acapulco a galleon unloaded its treasure onto wagons, which then traveled overland to ports on the Gulf of Mexico. There the cargo was reloaded on ships bound for Spain.

To protect its valuable cargo, a Manila galleon mounted forty to eighty heavy guns. The most powerful was a thirty-two-pounder. At close range it could send iron shot the size of coconuts smashing through two feet of solid oak.

Rogers knew a galleon was a floating fortress. "These large ships are built at Manila with excellent timber that will not splinter. They have very thick sides, much stronger than we build in Europe."

He also knew that, years earlier, a Manila galleon had fought off a fleet of fourteen Dutch privateers. The galleon sailed victoriously away from the battle, ninety cannonballs embedded like raisins in its hull. The defeated Dutch fleet slunk away with broken masts, torn sails, and seawater pouring through holes from the galleon's cannonballs in their sides.

By mid-December the galleon had still not arrived. The patrols went ceaselessly on, day after day. The *Marquiss* had to leave the picket line for repairs. She sailed for Port Segura (probably today's San Lucas on the southern tip of Baja California). The tiny Spanish settlement offered a harbor protected from wind and waves. Cannons on the *Marquiss* probably assured repairs could be carried out peacefully. The *Duke* and *Duchess* maintained the patrol, sailing back and forth, keeping watch.

On December 21 at nine o'clock in the morning, a lookout on the *Duke* cried, "A sail!" There she was, the Manila galleon, heading south for Acapulco, white sails bending to the wind, proud and bold.

Selkirk in the *Joseph* began tracking the lumbering treasure ship, staying just out of range of the big guns. Using signal lanterns at night, he kept the *Duke* and *Duchess* informed of the galleon's position. Rogers recorded: "[The] Duchess pass'd by her at night, and she fired 2 shot at [the galleon] but they return'd none."

In the morning Rogers gathered the crew around the mainmast and led them in prayer. Cups of hot chocolate were then distributed from a kettle on deck—the *Duke* had run out of rum. The same ceremony was taking place on the far-off *Duchess*, but she was becalmed. No wind moved her toward the galleon.

Sighting the galleon through his spyglass, Rogers saw "barrels hanging at each yard-arm, that looked like powder barrels, to deter us from boarding 'em. About 8 a clock we began to engage her by our selves."

Rogers's smaller and faster *Duke* came up behind, firing cannon shot into the galleon's stern, aiming at the exposed rudder, which steered the huge ship. The galleon replied with two small cannons mounted on the rail—stern chasers—but their aim was off. No shots hit the charging raider.

Rogers then drove the *Duke* along the big ship's side. Cannonballs splintered the *Duke's* deck, but the Spanish gunners "did not ply their great guns half as fast as we did."

Sharpshooters high in the *Duke's* rigging picked off Spanish gunners on the galleon's deck.

After a three-hour battle the galleon's flag suddenly dropped. Surrender!

A crew from *Duke* boarded the galleon. They found the Spanish sailors, after their six-month cruise from Manila, suffering from scurvy. Food and water were scarce. The *Duke's* boarding party herded the crew below decks, then worked the big galleon to Port Segura. The *Duke,* the *Duchess,* and Selkirk's *Joseph* followed. They found the *Marquiss* finishing repairs.

Nine Spanish seamen had been killed in the battle, ten wounded, "and several blown up and burnt with powder." But on *Duke* only two had been wounded. One was Rogers. A bullet from a Spanish sharpshooter had hit his left jaw.

"[The] bullet struck away a great part of my upper jaw and several of my teeth, part of which dropt upon the deck, where I fell."

The musket ball, the size of a grape, lodged sharp as a thorn in his jaw. Days later he swallowed a piece of jawbone, but the musket ball stayed in place.

Rogers chose Selkirk to accompany him aboard the galleon—the Spanish name recorded by Rogers as *Nostra Seniora de la Incarnacion Disenganio*—to inspect the treasure ship's cargo.

Both men were astonished at what they found: chests of gold coins; silver plates and wine goblets; belts of pearls; necklaces of rubies and diamonds; statues of gold and jade; delicate porcelain vases; tapestries to hang on the cold stone walls of palaces; silk gowns and stockings; swords with handles studded with precious gems; rolls of silk; tons of spices; caskets of earrings, bracelets, uncut gems; and more.

The cargo would bring a fabulous price in London. Rather than transfer the loot to the smaller ships,

Rogers decided to sail the *Incarnación*—renamed the *Batchelor*—back to England. For the 19,000-mile voyage he named Selkirk the ship's pilot.

On January 11, 1710, the four ships—the *Duke, Duchess, Marquiss,* and *Batchelor*—left Port Segura and headed west across the Pacific. (Rogers gave the smaller *Joseph* and *Increase* to the Spanish prisoners to sail to Acapulco.) No one knew in those years just how long a passage across the world's broadest ocean would take. One hundred miles noon to noon, the pace of a steady walk, was considered a good day's sail.

The first landfall, on March 11, was Guam. After 6,000 miles, the food was "almost exhausted."

Guam was a Spanish island. To persuade the governor to sell food to English ships, Rogers ordered gun ports opened. Cannon muzzles showed that the visitor was not to be trifled with. Rogers then wrote a letter to the island's governor:

"We . . . will not molest the settlement, provided you deal friendly by us. We will pay for whatever provisions and refreshments you have to spare. . . . But if after this civil request you deny us . . . you may immediately expect such military treatment, as we are with ease able to give you."

The governor was pleased to cooperate with "all imaginable friendship and respect."

In four days the ships took aboard 8 cows and calves, 60 pigs, 99 chickens, baskets of corn and yams, sacks of rice, 800 coconuts, limes, oranges, and melons, but, as far as is known, no green vegetables.

Rogers paid "double the value of what we received of them." Even in the enemy's camp his tact and courtesy showed.

The food, however, didn't last. So starved were the men during the passage from Guam west that they trapped rats in the holds—one rat skinned and cooked sold for sixpence. Rogers observed the crew eating the rodents "very savourly."

The lack of fresh food again brought on the seamen's sickness, scurvy—bleeding gums oozing pus, swollen limbs, dark moods, men too weak to leave their hammocks.

By June 20, when the ships arrived at Batavia (now

Jakarta) in the Dutch East Indies, seventy men on the four ships had died, mostly from the disease. Rogers sold the *Marquiss* for 575 Dutch dollars. Her bottom was "eat to a honey-comb by the worms." In places, only the thickness of a Spanish coin held the sea from entering the hull.

Still suffering his painful jaw wound, Rogers visited a Dutch doctor, who "cut a large musket-shot" out of his jaw, "which had been there near 6 months, ever since I was first wounded." A cup or two of rum to ease the pain was probably the only anesthesia he received.

For four months the crew recovered from the hardships of the Pacific crossing. Then the remaining three ships left the Dutch port. They sailed west across the Indian Ocean for the Cape of Good Hope on the southern tip of Africa.

On December 27 they anchored in Table Bay. Cape Town consisted of a church and 250 homes. Many showed fine gardens of flowers and grapevines. The *Duke* came sluggishly to rest. Water sloshed in her bottom. Pumps from the *Duchess* and *Batchelor* pumped her dry.

Three months later, on April 6, 1711, the *Duke, Duchess,* and *Batchelor* left Cape Town in a convoy of twenty-five Dutch merchant ships. The large fleet was a safety precaution against Spanish warships— England and Holland were still at war with Spain and France. The fleet arrived in the Dutch port of Texel on July 23.

For nearly three months the three privateers waited in Holland. Then four English warships arrived to bring them safely home.

Up the River Thames the *Duke* and *Duchess*, banners flying, escorted their valuable prize. They anchored two miles below London.

Rogers penned a final entry in his journal: "Octob. 14. This day at 11 of the clock, we and our consort and prize got up to Erith where we came to an anchor, which ends our long and fatiguing voyage."

Selkirk's grand adventure was over. There had been days on a faraway island when he had expected never to see England again. Wherever he looked now there were English warships, merchantmen, fishing smacks, the gold-trimmed barges of the wealthy. Life must have seemed very good.

"*[He] frequently bewailed his return to the world, which could not . . .
with all its enjoyments, restore him to the tranquility of his solitude.*"

Marooned in London

⮞

Selkirk had left London with little more than the clothes in his sea chest. Now, some eight years later, he returned to the city a wealthy man.

The sale of the treasure aboard the Manila galleon, the booty from twenty merchant ships, and the plunder from the raid on Guayaquil brought 147,975 pounds sterling (£). Investors—those wealthy merchants, lawyers, and physicians who, for £13,000, had bought the *Duke* and *Duchess* and provided the cannons, muskets, and cutlasses—took two-thirds of the profit. The remaining third was shared by the two crews according to rank and duties.

Rogers's share came to £1,600. Selkirk received £800, about the yearly income of a banker or leading merchant in London.

Each share was an enormous sum of money. Seamen on cargo ships typically earned one pound per month. A carpenter's wages for the same period amounted to a little more than two pounds, and plumbers received about four pounds a month for workdays that lasted ten to thirteen hours, six days a week.

Selkirk rented rooms in the home of John and Katherine Mason, a tailor and his wife. This would be his home for the next two and a half years. He slept in a feather bed under a thick comforter smelling of fresh herbs. He had money and good health, but he soon became restless and discontented.

On some mornings, half awake, he listened for the

clang of a ship's bell, the cries of the officer on watch, the *whoom* of sails catching wind. Instead, from the street came the rattle of wagons and coaches on paving stones, horses' hoofs clopping, dogs barking, the cries of vegetable sellers and knife grinders. Housemaids going about their duties padded by in the hall.

He may have wondered what a wealthy mariner back from a successful privateering voyage should do with his days. He had no need to find work. Like most newcomers to the city, he probably wandered. London's busy street life was always entertaining.

There were jugglers and acrobats to watch, as well as cockfights, dogfights, and sometimes a circle of men whipping a chained bear to the cheers of bystanders.

Taverns posted signs offering to make a man drunk for a penny. And there were games—cricket, tennis, bowling, and boxing matches between women as well as men. Peddlers playing hand organs offered rabbits for sale and pots of milk and water. Crowded streets often made way for firemen dashing to a burning house, hauling a water pump and shouting, "Hi! Hi! Hi!"

He may have visited the Wax Works, 140 lifelike figures of notable Londoners, and walked streets known for the occupations of merchants: goldsmiths in Guthron's Lane, butchers in East Cheap, shoemakers in Cordwainer Street, candlemakers in Lochbury.

On Mondays, Londoners hastened to hangings in the Tyburn district. Stands for spectators and a special gallows had been erected to send twenty-four men and women criminals to their just rewards at one drop. Tyburn was a popular public spectacle.

Days dawdled away. He strolled wharves where ships were loading and unloading. The waterfront was being filled in so wharves could be built to bring more goods—furs, wools, grain, beer, iron, wax, and more—for the city's growing population.

Selkirk was a reader, so no doubt he stopped at booksellers' shops and bought a daily newspaper to read in one of London's many coffeehouses. Shopkeepers, real estate agents, journalists, lawyers, and doctors sat at tables talking business and politics and smoking long clay pipes.

Everyone seemed to have a purpose, a destination,

an occupation. Selkirk's Scottish character urged that he account for each day with some useful work. He was free, but he needed an occupation.

When no other distraction offered itself and the day hung heavy, he found a tavern. There he whiled away hours drinking beer or ale and feeding his discontent with gin and brandy.

But his life was about to change.

Sometime in 1712 Woodes Rogers published a book.

A Cruising Voyage Round the World was an account of the privateering voyage Rogers had commanded. Sections told about the rescue of Selkirk on Juan Fernández and the capture of the Manila galleon.

The book became the most popular travel book of the year and was reprinted in French, Dutch, and German.

Selkirk, the man who had survived four years alone on an island, became a celebrity. Rogers escorted him about town and introduced him to rich friends. He was invited to dinner parties.

The former castaway, son of a leather tanner and harness maker, now entered an unfamiliar world of wealth and comfort. Rooms glowed with candles. The merchants, bankers, and ship owners Selkirk met wore clothes cut in the latest style—knee-length coats, frilled shirts, and vests of yellow, scarlet, or blue. Bright bows at the neck tied powdered wigs.

And the women—rare birds in tall hairdos, faces powdered and painted, pale arms untouched by sun. Gems sparkled in hair, around necks, on silken shoes. Their lively eyes watched the strange man who had lived on an uninhibited island.

Following Rogers's advice, Selkirk tried to talk about his four years alone. A brief mention that he wore a jacket and breeches of goatskin, however, likely brought on helpless laughter, itching and scratching, the elegant guests pretending the prickly skins touched their flesh.

Interest soon faded from their eyes. What they really wanted to hear about was the Manila galleon and all those lovely things the treasure ship had carried—gold and silver plates and wine goblets, silk stockings and gowns, swords with handles of precious gems, and more.

He was a merely an amusement, a novelty to occupy an idle hour.

Dinner was usually not served until nine o'clock— soup and fish and meat and fowl, twelve courses in all.

Should he say he had chased goats over rocks to put food in his stomach? Had watched shipmates skin and cook rats to eat? It sounded unreal. How could they understand hunger, how it made good men mean and savage?

In most homes when dinner ended, guests moved to the drawing room. Servants set up tables and the card games began—loo and faro and hazard.

The games often lasted until dawn lightened the sky. The air was then thick with pipe smoke and the women's heavy perfume. Too much brandy might have left his head woolly.

Selkirk may have found himself standing alone at a tall window overlooking a garden, perhaps thinking back to dawns on his island, the sun rising out of the Pacific, the air cool, Great Bay reflecting high pink clouds.

Then, out of the blue, a chance came to return to his island. A meeting with Woodes Rogers offered the possibility.

The former privateer captain now dressed in the latest fashion—scarlet coat with brass buttons, velvet breeches, black silk stockings, a wig with curls that hung to his shoulders. He had become a successful businessman, sending merchant ships loaded with cargo to the Bahama Islands, east of Florida. (In 1717 King George I was to appoint Rogers "Captain-General and Governor-in-Chief in and over our Bahama Islands in America.")

Now that peace had been restored between England and Spain, Rogers told his former mate and comrade, a new, highly profitable venture was in the works. The South Sea Company was the idea of Sir Robert Harley, Chancellor of the Exchequer, the royal treasury. The plan was to set up trading posts along the coastal towns of South America. Rogers would be the expedition leader.

The project was big, exciting! A fleet of twenty warships—including one with eighty guns—forty cargo ships, five hospital ships, four thousand soldiers. Juan Fernández would become a supply depot. Selkirk knew the island best. Would he help set up the colony? The South Seas Company had already spent £120,000, and the Secretary of State, Henry St. John, had pledged even more government money. Investors were pouring in additional funds. Even Queen Anne was interested.

Weeks later, Rogers again met with Selkirk. His news was disappointing. Funds from the government were not coming—no, he didn't know why, no one did. It was a huge scandal. Thousands of investors had lost money. The South Seas Company was bankrupt. There would be no ships, no soldiers, no supply depot on Juan Fernández. Queen Anne and all those high government officials refused to say what had happened.

For Selkirk, any hope he might have had of returning to his island home was now gone.

Rogers also introduced Selkirk to Richard Steele, a journalist who had helped Rogers write his book. After hearing about Selkirk and reading Rogers's book, Steele wanted to tell the castaway's story on Juan Fernández for his magazine, *The Englishman*.

"I had the pleasure frequently to converse with the man soon after his arrival in England in the year 1711. It was a matter of great curiosity to hear him, as he is a man of good sense, give an account of . . . that long solitude."

Steele was a member of Parliament, heavyset and limping with gout. He and Selkirk met in coffeehouses. Soon Steele saw that the former castaway seemed uneasy with his new life in London.

"[He] frequently bewailed his return to the world," Steele wrote, "which could not . . . with all its enjoyments, restore him to the tranquility of his solitude" on his island.

"I am now worth 800 pounds," the despondent mariner told him, "but shall never be so happy as when I was not worth a farthing."

On that far-off island, Steele wrote, Selkirk's "life grew so exquisitely pleasant that he never had a moment heavy upon his hands. His nights were untroubled and his days joyous from the practice of temperance and exercise. . . . His life was one continual feast."

Selkirk's story took up the entire December 1–3, 1713, issue of *The Englishman*.

Watching the glum mariner sip coffee, Steele realized what troubled the former castaway: He yearned for his island home.

Wearing a handsome blue waistcoat with white cuffs and lapels and a cocked hat, the new lieutenant boarded his ship.

Largo and Beyond

⌒

*T*n the spring of 1714 Selkirk left London for Largo. He hadn't seen his mother and father in ten, almost eleven years. Were they still alive?

The trip in a rattling coach was about 400 miles over rutted roads, so he most likely took passage on a coastal trader. At Edinburgh he would have changed to a ferry to cross the fifteen-mile-wide mouth of the Firth of Forth.

Herring boats bobbing in the quiet water of Largo

Bay, same as when he was a boy, was probably his first sight of home. The seaside village on that Sunday morning had not changed. The same stone houses with thatched roofs; stairways to second floors on outside walls; iron weathervanes, mostly fish, pointing nowhere. Behind the houses, sheep grazed on sloping hills.

For his homecoming, Selkirk wore a new coat with gold trim. He was barbered and groomed. He walked up the path to the family cottage. The longed-for moment was finally here. He opened the door, stepped into the kitchen, ready to hug his old mother, give his dad a manly embrace.

But the kitchen was empty. A low fire probably flickered in the hearth and fresh bread and cake waited on the table. But the house was still. Then he remembered: The day was Sunday.

Up the path he strode past the churchyard, where stood headstones of departed grandparents, aunts, and cousins. He stepped into the Presbyterian church, still stone cool. The congregation was singing a hymn. He knew the words. He had sung the same in this church as a boy and on a far-off island as a man.

What happened next became part of the family legend. It was retold years later by his cousin John Howell.

"As soon as he sat down, all eyes were upon him, for such a personage perhaps had seldom been seen within the church at Largo. He was elegantly dressed in gold-laced clothes. Besides, he was a stranger, which in a country church is a matter of attention at all times.

"After remaining some time engaged in devotion, his eyes were ever turning to where his parents and brothers sat, while theirs as often met his gaze. Still, they did not know him.

"At length, his mother recognized him and, uttering a cry of joy, could contain herself no longer. Even in the house of God she rushed to his arms, unconscious of the impropriety of her conduct and the interruption of the service.

"Alexander and the family's friends immediately retired to his father's house to give free scope to their joy and congratulations."

The gathering must have been typical of the day: aunts, uncles, cousins crowding the door; neighbors who remembered Alexander as a wee lad peering through windows; fishermen he had gone sailing with stopping by; boys he had played with, now men, sitting with wives, sipping tea, eating buttered bread. His old teacher, bent with age, who remembered him as a bright but at times unruly pupil, telling all who would listen that Alexander had shown little interest in his books except for mathematics and geometry. The rooms loud with the babble of talk and sudden whoops of laughter.

There were brother John and his wife, Margaret, and brother David. There was also Andrew, his feeble-minded brother, now a grown man.

Euphan, his mother, lingered nearby. For the celebration she most likely served haggis, a special pudding for holidays, made from the heart, liver, and other organs of a sheep.

But for Alexander the joy of homecoming lasted only a few days. The questions, the stares, the hearty slaps on the back soon began to get on his nerves. He became uncomfortable with hovering cousins, aunts, old school chums, well-meaning neighbors.

He tried to be polite, to listen. In all likelihood his family and friends talked about matters of little interest to him—the herring catch, the church's need for a new roof, squabbles with the next village over grass for the sheep. This was their world, the world of Largo.

To escape the press of company, he spent days along Largo Bay talking with fishermen. He bought a boat and went sailing. On the open water he was alone. At Kingscraig Point, under the cliff at low tide, he caught lobsters and brought them home for the evening meal.

Worried about his moody son, his father probed gently. Was he ready to settle down, join him in the shop—leather tanning and shoemaking—perhaps take a village girl to wife?

It was his father's old wish, his heartfelt plea. But Alexander didn't fit in Largo. He was a stranger here. The village was too small—about 1,200 lived in the cluster of houses. The people, his parents included, were too narrow, too set in their ways, for a traveled man who had seen a larger world.

He moved out of his parents' house and took an upstairs room in the home of his brother John and his wife, Margaret. Perhaps a change of living arrangements would help.

For breakfast, Margaret usually served porridge, a tattie—potato—and a mug of tea with milk and sugar. Alexander likely stood while eating his porridge, following a belief of the time: standing aided digestion.

After breakfast, probably carrying a wrapping of bread and dried fish for a noon meal, he took long walks in the wooded hills and to Keil's Den, where the ruins of Pitcruvie Castle stood. Returning at dark, he took the outside steps to his second-floor room and avoided neighbors and cousins waiting on the first floor.

Margaret kept two cats. She watched while Alexander held the forelegs of one, hummed a tune, and tried to teach it to dance. This-way, that-way, take-a-step, take-a-step. When the animal tripped over its hind feet, Alexander became annoyed. Margaret told her husband about his brother's strange behavior.

Then Alexander did something that astonished everyone.

With a spade he began enlarging a cave on the side of a hill in Keil's Den. He installed boards to support the roof. In front he scraped a flat place and cobbled together a bench. Villagers passing on the lane below saw him sitting on the bench, chin on hands, staring across the bay.

His worried parents trudged up the slope. The found their son weeping. "Oh, my beloved island!" he blubbered helplessly. "I wish I had never left thee. I never was before the man I was on thee. And I fear never can be again."

A grown man crying! John and Euphan didn't know what to make of it. Such sadness in his eyes. They may have tried to console him, assuring him he had aunts and uncles and cousins who loved him, brothers and friends, too.

Likely his father urged him again to come work in the shop, anytime, even tomorrow! A place would be made for him.

Euphan may have tried reaching out to her son but saw he was beyond comforting.

Soon came the day when Alexander left. He gave a boy a penny to follow with his sea chest on a cart. John and Euphan watched as he walked down the hill. Father and mother may have felt a sense of farewell, something telling them they would never see their son again.

At the bay he boarded the ferry to Edinburgh. There he would find a ship to London.

In late 1716 or early 1717 he enlisted in the Royal Navy. He was assigned to H.M.S. *Enterprise*, a supply ship.

By November 1720 Selkirk had been promoted to master's mate, second in command. The rank just below captain, master's mate, or lieutenant, was the highest rank someone not of the upper class could attain.

Wearing a handsome blue waistcoat with white cuffs and lapels and a cocked hat, the new lieutenant boarded his ship, H.M.S. *Weymouth*, at Plymouth. Together with H.M.S. *Swallow*, the warship headed for West Africa to hunt pirates and slave traders. The sun off the coast was intense, nights humid without a breeze.

In June 1721 Selkirk sent a boat up the Gambia River to find fresh water and cut wood for the cook stove. The crew was captured by natives. Boats filled with musket-carrying seamen from the *Weymouth* went to find the missing men in the mosquito-infested jungle. The rescued crew members returned to the ship bringing with them a deadly sickness, most likely malaria or yellow fever.

Disease swept through the *Weymouth*. Each day fewer crew answered morning roll call. Men began dying.

Sometime in November or December, Selkirk became ill. The ship's doctor placed him in a hammock slung from beams in the captain's cabin, which had been turned into a hospital ward.

Medicine at the time knew little about treating tropical diseases. The doctor did what he could to ease the men's suffering—cooling their flushed faces with water-soaked cloths, offering a thin soup to settle nausea, massaging aching limbs, placing blankets on feverish bodies shivering with cold, wiping away vomited blood, pouring cups of water between trembling lips that still left thirst unsatisfied.

On December 13, 1721, the *Weymouth*'s captain entered a new name in the ship's log:

Alexr. Selkirk, DD . . . P.M.

"DD" stood for "today's date" written at the top of the page. "P.M." meant death occurred some hour between noon and midnight.

As was the practice, Selkirk's body was enclosed in a sack made from an old sail. The sack was weighted with two cannonballs, one at the head and one at the feet. Then it was placed on a plank and lifted onto the ship's rail.

The captain read the old words of the burial service from The Book of Common Prayer. "Deliver your servant, Alexander . . . from all evil, and set him free from every bond. . . . "

The plank was tilted, and Selkirk's body slid into the gray waves somewhere off the coast of Africa.

H.M.S. *Weymouth* returned to England in 1722. Lieutenant Selkirk's sea chest was sent to Largo. There it joined the few belongings he had left behind at his brother's house—a gold-laced coat, a brown stoneware flip jar, a clam shell he had once used to dip cool water from a turtle shell in a hut on an island some ten thousand miles away, and a musket.

The stock of the musket was carved with a picture and a rhyme. During an idle afternoon the marooned mariner had engraved his name, a seal on a rock, and these words:

> With 3 drams powder
> 3 ounce hail

Ram me well & prime me
To kill I will not fail.

"Hail" referred to a hail of bullets.

On a high hill on Juan Fernández today stands a bronze tablet. The spot is called Selkirk's Lookout. There the lonely castaway stacked dry grass and firewood and watched with his brass spyglass for a rescue ship. The tablet was placed by the officers of a British warship, H.M.S. *Topaze*, in 1863 and reads:

In memory of Alexander Selkirk, mariner, a native of Largo, in the county of Fife, Scotland, who lived on this island in complete solitude for four years and four months. He was landed from the Cinque Ports galley, 96 tons, A.D. 1704, was taken off in the Duke, privateer, 12th Feb., 1709. He died Lieutenant of H.M.S. Weymouth A.D. 1728, aged 47 years.

The last date was incorrect. The *Weymouth*'s logbook in the Public Records Office in London gives 1721 as the year of his passing. He was 41.

Still, the tablet, erected nearly a century and a half after Selkirk's death, recognized the Scottish mariner's magnificent adventure—a salute to a fellow seaman who had survived four years alone on a remote island in the broad ocean sea.

"I was born in the year 1632, in the city of York, of a good family. . . ."

The Real Robinson Crusoe

☙

*T*here was a man in London who had read Woodes Rogers's *Cruising Voyage Around the World* and Richard Steele's account of Selkirk's years on Juan Fernández in *The Englishman*.

Daniel Defoe was a failed businessman. At the time Rogers's and Steele's accounts of Selkirk's adventures came out in 1712 and 1713, he was in his early fifties. Short of money, he was trying to pay off debts, support a wife and children, and maintain a big house by writing books, pamphlets, and newspaper articles.

Defoe had a sharp tongue. His political stories annoyed men in high positions in the church and government. He was a gadfly, constantly nagging them with criticism. One of his pamphlets, published around 1700, charged some members of Parliament with disrespect for the rights of Englishmen. The powerful men he named did not appreciate his views. A £50 reward was offered for his capture.

The London Gazette described the fugitive—the only description we have of Defoe. "He is middle aged, a spare man, about forty years old, of a brown complexion, dark-colored hair, but wears a wig. A hooked nose, a sharp chin, gray eyes, a large mole near his mouth."

An informer turned him in for the reward. The government charged him with sedition—urging people to resist new laws. Defoe spent the next six months in Newgate Prison and was fined £135.

As much as he wrote through the years, by his sixtieth year Defoe was tired and broke, partly because he made unwise investments in business ventures that didn't turn profits.

Creditors badgered him for money he had borrowed. What he needed was a big score, a money-maker. He remembered Rogers's book and Steele's account of Selkirk's marooning. Here was the story he was looking for, a man surviving alone on an uninhabited island.

But there was a flaw in the idea. In the early eighteenth century almost all books published were nonfiction. Histories, biographies, and travel books were popular subjects. Novels rarely appeared.

Defoe, though, did not want to let the idea go. He spoke with his printer, W. T. Taylor in Pater Noster Row. They agreed that a book about a marooned sea-man on a tropical island might sell, but only if it read like nonfiction, if it seemed factual, not a story.

How to do this? A clever idea presented itself. The hero should write the book himself, make the story appear as though it had really happened.

In April 1719 the new book appeared in the shops of London booksellers. Defoe's name did not appear as author. The title page read: *The Life and Strange Surprizing Adventures of Robinson Crusoe, of York, Mariner. Written by Himself.*

"I was born in the year 1632, in the city of York, of a good family. . . . "

These opening lines begin what is probably the most famous adventure story ever told, the tale of the shipwrecked mariner who survived twenty-eight years on an island off Brazil. The book is still available today in bookstores and libraries almost three hundred years after it was first published.

Readers believed Crusoe's story was true. In the Preface, Defoe noted that the book was "a just history of fact; neither is there any appearance of fiction in it."

W. T. Taylor printed 1,500 copies of *Robinson Crusoe*. So popular was the new book that it was reprinted a month later, again in June, and twice more by the end of the year. In October the story was serialized in *The Original London Post* for sixty-five weeks, an astonishing run.

Defoe never named Selkirk as the model for his hero. But in a new edition of his novel he wrote:

There is a man alive, and well known too, the actions of whose life are [my] subject, and to whom all or most part of the story alludes: this may be depended upon for the truth, and to this I set my name.

Defoe's notes for his story, still preserved in the Guildhall Library in London, read in part: "Goats plenty. Fish: abundance, split and salt. . . . The fat of young seals good as olive oil."

There is also mention of a visit with a Captain Thomas Bowry of the East India Company, a shipping firm. Bowry showed Defoe maps of Juan Fernández.

Ten years after it was published, Defoe's story appeared in French, and by 1760 in German, Dutch, and Russian. Translations appear today in nearly all the world's languages.

After the success of the first Crusoe story, Defoe wrote two more: *Further Adventures of Robinson Crusoe* in 1719 and *Serious Reflections of Robinson Crusoe* the next year. These books, however, never attracted readers of the original story and have been largely forgotten.

In his lifetime, Defoe turned out an awesome amount of writing, possibly as many as 566 separate works—novels, long poems, political pamphlets, articles for 27 newspapers and magazines, and between 250 and 300 books. Besides *Crusoe,* his *Moll Flanders* (1722) remains in print today.

Despite his outpouring of words, Defoe never seemed to earn enough money to support his wife and seven children in their big house in Stoke Newington. In April 1731 he was hiding from people he owed money to in a shabby rooming house in Ropemaker's Alley in London. There he died, some twelve years after his famous novel first appeared.

In *Robinson Crusoe,* Defoe created one of the most enduring characters in all fiction.

Did Selkirk ever read the story? Possibly. In April 1719, when the novel appeared, he was on leave from H.M.S. *Enterprise* and in London. On daily walks about the city he sometimes visited bookstores. We can only wonder if he picked up the book, paged through it, and recalled once more the island paradise he had known.

At the end of his famous story, Defoe arranged for

Crusoe to return to the island on which he had lived for twenty-eight years. But we know that was only fiction. Alexander Selkirk, the real-life Robinson Crusoe, never found his island home again.

Author's Note

I came upon Selkirk's story about twenty years ago. In a used-book store in New York I found a copy of *The Fabulous Originals: Lives of Extraordinary People Who Inspired Memorable Characters in Fiction.* The book was written by Irving Wallace and published in 1955.

In the chapter titled "The Real Robinson Crusoe," Wallace wrote about the Scottish seaman marooned on Juan Fernández in 1704, how he survived, and his rescue four years and four months later. The story was fascinating, and I began to look for more books about Alexander Selkirk and his strange adventure.

Woodes Rogers, John Howell, and Richard Steele, all mentioned in Wallace's account, became the primary sources of information about him. Rogers and Steele knew Selkirk personally; Howell, a century after Selkirk's death, recorded family stories about his boyhood and later years.

Rogers's *A Cruising Voyage Round the World*, published in London in 1712, was reprinted in 1970 and can be found in bookstores today.

An unexpected discovery—luck, really—led me to Howell's *The Life and Adventures of Alexander Selkirk,* published in Scotland in 1829. My town library was skeptical about finding a book so old but nevertheless agreed to search for it.

Amazingly, it was found within a week. The University of

Minnesota's Wilson Library in Minneapolis, about thirty-five miles from my home, had an original copy.

The librarian in the hushed rare books room carried the worn volume in two hands and set it gently on the table before me. There I read about the Selcraigs—for some unknown reason, Selkirk changed his last name before boarding the *Cinque Ports*—who lived in a seacoast village in Scotland some 300 years ago. I was surprised to read that family life for the Selcraigs was not all that different from family life today.

Although I couldn't locate the December 1–3, 1713, issue of *The Englishman*—the paper was published for only three years—I found excerpts from Steele's talks with Selkirk in Wallace's book and in other sources listed in the Selected Bibliography. The British Library—the national library of Great Britain—would be a likely place to start a search for the original 1713 issue.

The primary sources mentioned above—Rogers, Howell, and Steele—told Selkirk's story. Rogers wrote about the marooned mariner's days on Juan Fernández, his role in the capture of the Manila galleon, and his celebrity in London. Howell told of his return home to Largo, his inability to fit into village life, and his decision to leave parents and family for the last time. Steele interviewed the former castaway about his island home and his yearning to return there.

Irving Wallace in *The Fabulous Originals* provided an overview of Selkirk's life and showed how his marooning on Juan Fernández provided Daniel Defoe with the basis for his famous novel, *Robinson Crusoe*.

The last book I read was especially helpful. *A Pirate of Exquisite Mind: Explorer, Naturalist, and Buccaneer: The Life of William Dampier* by Diana and Michael Preston, published in

2004, tells how seventeenth- and eighteenth-century mariners sailed the unexplored South Pacific Ocean, and provides a colorful background to Selkirk's adventures.

To become acquainted with Selkirk and his life and times, I read twenty-three books, some all the way through, others only in part.

Most of the books came from or through my local public library. Those not in the library's collection were borrowed from other libraries.

Librarians are always most helpful in research of this kind. Their suggestions often led to sources of information I would otherwise have never known about.

Juan Fernández has changed much since Selkirk's day.

About 1966 the government of Chile changed the name from Juan Fernández to Robinson Crusoe Island. It was hoped the name change would attract more tourists to the island. A second island a hundred miles to the west was renamed Alejendro [Alexander] Selkirk Island, although Selkirk never visited it.

Five hundred people today live on Robinson Crusoe, but Alejendro Selkirk is uninhabited, except for fishermen who spend summer months there harvesting lobsters. The lobsters on both islands are smaller today than the three-footers Selkirk caught.

San Juan Bautista on Cumberland Bay (the Great Bay of Selkirk's day) is a village of modest homes with yards lush with roses, sunflowers, and geraniums. Visitors find a post office, three small hotels, shops selling Crusoe and Selkirk souvenirs, but no hospital, pharmacy, or bank—or taxes. Most men on the island leave early each morning to tend lobster traps in the bay.

TV arrived on Robinson Crusoe in 1986 and telephones in 1993. A monthly supply boat from Valparaiso, Chile—360 miles due east on "the continent," as South America is called—brings fresh vegetables, building supplies, and gas for fishing boats and for the few cars on the island.

In summer the boat also delivers supplies to Alejendro Selkirk Island and picks up live lobsters for restaurants on the mainland.

About 120 students are enrolled in Robinson Crusoe's only school, kindergarten through eighth grade. Ninth-grade students attend school in Valparaiso. A Chilean naval ship transports the boys and girls in March and returns them to the island at Christmas.

Most of the island today is a Chilean national park. Sixty percent of its plants—among them 20 species of ferns and 131 kinds of moss—are found nowhere else in the world. Rare birds include the brick-red firecrown hummingbird.

Sheep, cows, and goats graze hillsides now cleared of the forests where Selkirk once roamed. El Yunque —"the anvil"— rises above the village. At 3,002 feet, the summit is often hidden by clouds.

To visit the island requires a three-hour flight from Santiago, Chile. The plane lands on a red-dirt airstrip—the only flat stretch on the mountainous island. Visitors then travel for six miles by boat to San Juan Bautista.

Wooden signs along paths direct visitors to Selkirk's cave and to Selkirk's Lookout, the high ridge where the marooned mariner watched for ships, and to the tablet left by H.M.S. *Topaze* in 1863. Seals still bask on rocky beaches below steep cliffs fronting the bay.

Glossary

barnacle   A shellfish that attaches itself to objects underwater, such as rocks, whales, or a ship's bottom.

bilge   The curved inside bottom of a ship's hull. (See *hull*.)

boarding ax   A handle with a blade similar to that of today's ax, used as a weapon when boarding a merchant vessel and also to cut lines supporting sails to disable the ship.

bow   The front end of a boat or ship.

capstan   A thick rotating drum for winding up a rope or chain attached to an anchor.

careen   To heel or tip a boat or ship on its side to clean or repair the outer hull.

cutlass   A short, heavy sword with a slightly curved blade and a single cutting edge.

Drake, Sir Francis   English admiral, navigator, and pirate who sailed around the world, 1577–80.

farthing   A coin in use in the seventeenth and eighteenth centuries, worth about one-quarter of a penny.

flintlock   A firearm—usually a musket—that has a piece of flint striking against steel to produce sparks. The sparks ignite gunpowder in the musket's barrel, which drives a bullet through the barrel. (See *musket*.)

galleon   A large Spanish sailing vessel of the fifteenth to seventeenth centuries, used as a fighting ship or a merchant ship.

grappling hook   Three or more curved pieces of metal, shaped like fishhooks, attached to a line thrown from an attacking ship to grasp the railing of a merchant ship to draw that ship close to the attacker.

hull   The basic outer frame of a ship that supports decks, masts, and sails.

longboat   A service boat; the longest boat carried on the deck of a sailing ship, powered by two or more oarsmen when lowered into the water.

mariner   A sailor, a seaman.

maroon   To put ashore and abandon a person on a deserted island by way of punishment.

mast   A long upright pole—originally the trunk of a tree shorn of branches—that supports a ship's sails, yardarms, rigging, etc. Most sailing ships in Selkirk's day had two masts.

mate   The ranking first, second, or third officer on a ship, under the captain.

merchantman   A trading ship; a ship carrying cargo. Also called a *merchant ship*.

musket   A heavy gun with a long barrel introduced in the sixteenth century; the forerunner of the modern rifle. (See *flintlock*.)

oakum   Loose strands obtained by untwisting and picking apart old ropes, used to pack between planks of wooden ships.

Peru Current   A cold Pacific Ocean current flowing north along the coasts of Chile and Peru. Also called the Humboldt Current.

pirate   An outlaw in an armed ship unlawfully attacking merchant ships of all countries and ransacking coastal towns. Also called a *buccaneer*.

pitch   A dark, tarry substance used to waterproof seams between planks on wooden ships.

pound   English unit of currency.

powder barrel   A container filled with gunpowder. It was fastened to the side rigging of a pirate ship or privateer, the fuse lighted, and the barrel released to explode on the deck of an adjoining ship.

privateer A merchant ship, privately owned, fitted with guns, and commissioned by a government to attack enemy merchantmen in wartime. (During the Revolutionary War 1,600 American privateers captured 1,000 British merchantmen.)

sailing master The second or third officer after the captain; often the navigator who steers the ship between ports.

scurvy A disease caused by lack of vitamin C in the diet. Victims suffer bleeding gums, loose teeth, weakness of limbs, and internal bleeding. Often fatal when untreated.

spyglass A small telescope.

stern The rear end of a boat or ship.

teredo worm A worm equipped with two small-toothed shells on its head. It burrows into oak timbers on a ship's hull, threatening a ship's safety. Also called *shipworm*.

tiller A horizonal bar or lever attached to the rudder of a small boat for steering the boat.

War of the Spanish Succession A war, 1701–1714, in which England, Austria, and the Netherlands fought Spain, France, and Prussia in a dispute over who should become king after Spain's Charles II died.

yard, yardarm A long wooden pole attached crosswise from a mast to support a sail.

Selected Bibliography

Backscheider, Paula R. *Daniel Defoe: His Life.* Baltimore, Md.: Johns Hopkins University Press, 1989.

Botting, Douglas, and the Editors of Time-Life Books. *The Pirates.* Alexandria, Va.: Time-Life Books, 1978.

National Geographic Society. *Islands Lost in Time.* Washington, D.C.: The National Geographic Society, 1997.

Defoe, Daniel. *The Life and Adventures of Robinson Crusoe.* Baltimore, Md.: Penguin Books, 1965.

Howell, John. *The Life and Adventures of Alexander Selkirk.* Edinburgh, Scotland: Oliver & Boyd, 1829.

MacLiesh, Fleming, and Martin L. Krieger. *The Privateers: A Raiding Voyage on the Great South Sea.* New York: Random House, 1962.

Preston, Diana, and Michael Preston. *A Pirate of Exquisite Mind: Explorer, Naturalist, and Buccaneer: The Life of William Dampier.* New York: Walker & Company, 2004.

Quennell, Peter. "The Man Who Was Robinson Crusoe." In *Condé Nast Traveler,* May 1990.

Rogers, Woodes. *A Cruising Voyage Round the World.* New York: Dover Publications, 1970.

Schurz, William. *The Manila Galleon.* New York: E. P. Dutton & Company, 1939.

Simmons, James. "Alexander Selkirk: The Monarch of Juan Fernández Island." In *Oceans,* March 1982.

Souhami, Diana. *Selkirk's Island: The True and Strange Adventures of the Real Robinson Crusoe.* New York: Harcourt, 2001.

Wallace, Irving. *The Fabulous Originals: Lives of Extraordinary People Who Inspired Memorable Characters in Fiction.* New York: Alfred A. Knopf, 1955.

Index